SURVIVOR'S NOTEBOOK

poems

SURVIVOR'S
NOTEBOOK

DAN O'BRIEN

ACRE

CINCINNATI 2023

Acre Books is made possible by the support of the Robert and Adele Schiff Foundation and the Department of English at the University of Cincinnati.

ISBN-13 (pbk) 978-1-946724-63-2
ISBN-13 (ebook) 978-1-946724-64-9

Designed by Barbara Neely Bourgoyne
Cover photographs: Dan O'Brien
Cover design: Barbara Neely Bourgoyne

Photo credits on page 97 are a continuation of the copyright page.

The press is based at the University of Cincinnati, Department of English and Comparative Literature, Arts & Sciences Hall, Room 248, PO Box 210069, Cincinnati, OH, 45221-0069.

Acre Books books may be purchased at a discount for educational use. For information please email business@acre-books.com.

For Jessica, and for Bebe

CONTENTS

spring

Good Friday

Put under, my sins resected, and pulled back up again. Easter morning,
I imagined, but really it was the veiled day, the muzzled hours, waking
to my hummingbird of a heartbeat while my daughter leapt elsewhere,
barefoot from stone to mud; friends doing what they could to mother
in place of my wife, who wept beside her father in the hall. Time is
resuming, and despite my daughter's cold this morning I cry for joy
when she cannot see.

Toothbrush

You bought it for me: manual, the kind we used as children. The kind
you required after your bilateral mastectomy in the fall: feathery bristles
as our oncologists suggested. To spare the gums that bleed more freely
from the anticoagulants, the chemotherapy. Already you were sharing
the tools of your trade. Our trade now. Calling your name in the night
in my fever hallucinating, heaving. You held the glinting kidney dish
beneath my chin. Then, when it was over, you brought the toothbrush
to my lips.

The Nurse

She sudsed my penis briskly without apparent shame as I sat shivering
upon the high white throne. Passing black. Seven inches of bowel gone.
During those thirteen days she was the only one with enough—what,
callousness?—to acknowledge the squalor of my sex, and in particular
the glans the catheter tube split so obscenely. While making small talk
with my wife. Nobody rinsed me; the nurse said it was good to wrench
my sutured belly to the sink and mirror howling grasping learning again
how to care for myself.

Sunday

O may it be Sunday always and everywhere in California. Blemishless women with breathless cheekbones wavering in line for coffee. My girl in the back seat, her mother beside me. Unseen whistling for the tabby as coyotes lope through alleys; we park downslope. Bowers garlanded in blush. I press my daughter's body to my body and carry her through the chlorine cavity. Beneath polluted arteries. The enlarging bright aperture of sand. Then waves that pain my feet: my senseless skin revivifying in the effluvial flop and stream. I am becoming less and more myself. Renascent. The mountain snows dribble from a drainage pipe like the seminal Jordan. Seagulls alight as if to say, *Look where you are standing. For this you have survived.* Our daughter laughs as she pummels us both. O may it be always and everywhere now.

After the Scan

On the bench the discarded gown the unwound shroud in the empty tomb

The Prayer Is the Protagonist

Rejoice without ceasing testing your lungs refrain retain may the God of peace mark you may you be preserved pardoned becalmed and trust the life that rhymes persuades

A Vision

A man is praying is the man a gardener on his knees his hands are his hands planting seeds weeding wind what is this man unlocking is it spring

Good Will

Because they remind me. The bed clothes and the sick clothes; but also the blue Jeans from New York, the shirt for the shoot for the opening of a play meant to mark the deep-sixing of my childhood. My middling martyrdom. Certain other articles I blame for the cancer—something to do with color. And outmoded attitudes with which I imbued a leather jacket, for example, like the skin of my ambition. Insulation against contempt. There was not enough heart in them. We are relatively secure; so I stuff them in trash bags. Drive to the rusted dumpster beside the bank, beside a disheveled man dozing on a derelict couch, and drop them in the clanging hole.

Fish Market

For two years like a chapter in somebody else's unpublishable memoir I lived in the East Village and daily went running even farther east from my illegal sublet through Alphabet City to the river and south beneath the Williamsburg, the Manhattan, then the Brooklyn Bridge and when I reached the Fulton Fish Market, the stalls and fish and men would all be long gone; just the leftover stink, the hosed-down asphalt sticky and steaming with ice melting in the shadows. I would hold my breath then breathe as shallowly as I could manage, basically hyperventilating until Battery Park and the illegal sublet where my girlfriend was living; where we'd wake up Tuesday morning to the sirens and the Tower on fire, and the next Tower hit as I dawdled on the street gawping. The stench in the air we took into our lungs was ash, glass, cinders, flesh, bone— what would one day give us cancer. But one can only hold one's breath so long. In the days after, I went running away from the market, north, but by then the damage was done.

Fire Escape

We were trying to sleep on the top floor while the party pounded below, when they started climbing the fire escape outside our window up to the roof to smoke, drink, flirt, gazing across the sequins of the city to the Hudson. Such entitlement! And after a while we couldn't take it any longer. So with the approach of the next tipsy reveler I sprang from the bed and banged on the window as he passed. He yelped—his glass free-falling into the courtyard below, shattering. "Shit!" he cried, clinging to the fire escape as it shook . . . "Shit, shit, shit." Then laughter from his friends above. The window had been sealed with some sort of insulating plastic by the previous tenant, so I was as blurry to him as he was to me. But fearing retaliation I did what any sane city dweller does and ranted in a gibberish. To scare him off. He climbed higher, giggling, *Shit . . . Shit . . .* "What would've happened if he fell?" my fiancée asked as I crawled back into bed. Little had gone wrong for us yet—my family disowning me; our cancers. I shrugged. Hands trembling. "Our lives would have changed forever," I said. But things stayed quiet for the rest of the night, and we slept.

Our Mother's Health

She seemed impregnable—to infection, at least; what with six children somebody was always coming down with something. She taught us that illness infiltrates and pervades; schools and supermarkets and subways though she rarely left the house. To be honest she and our father were recluses. They didn't have any friends. She would affect insouciance before telling us: "Go wash your hands just one more time." *Whose fault was it though?* That was the question; the source of every misfortune visited upon our household was the obsessive sore she compulsively probed. My brother's anguish. Her brother's madness. Her mother's drunken slaps. But she was not afraid, she'd proudly proclaim: "Mothers are inoculated by love." And it almost made sense. How she stayed well while her children were left to ask themselves her question now.

Carnivorous

Firstly a friend's birthday inside a repurposed caboose on cinderblocks in Valhalla (NY). Beneath Kensico Dam. Where John Cheever stalked the woods in search of hand jobs. Waiters, like priests in white aprons smeared and speckled with blood, served the lipid-flecked filet of gristle with the black-handled serrated knife. We sawed, bit the candy-seared flesh dolloped with ketchup. Then I was a teenager tending charcoal briquettes in our backyard. Pivoting to evade the puckering flames' fuming jets of char. I was both nourishing and poisoning, I knew that even then, as I offered the carcass on my parents' silver marriage platter to the liars around the table. Is it fate that I fell in love with a woman who promised to forgive my unhealthy appetites? I don't miss it, strangely; since my diagnosis I have almost entirely lost the taste.

Disaster

He was riding his tricycle. She was driving home from college in Utah for the summer and her friends survived (one became a Hall of Fame quarterback, the other a state judge). He was out walking the poodle one fine evening in Princeton, got pinned to a wall. She was an intern at a prestigious literary magazine when a cab in a crosswalk knocked out her sense of smell, resulting in a settlement and a brownstone near Washington Square. They were married less than a day when a spider on his shoulder flinched their rental car over the line into an oncoming bus. She had leukemia; she died. A brain tumor twenty-five years ago, a broken back last year, and she has survived. So many divorces, suicides during this, our latter-day adolescence. I was sixteen riding shotgun when my friend hit an African diplomat's son—scooped and slammed onto the hood, spat back into the road, his ten-speed crunching under our tires. He stood up. We stood around him, doors flung wide, dashboard pinging, engine idling. Radio on. We could not understand a word he was saying.

Funny

I used to be. When I was a kid I might find myself on a roll in company and it would almost frighten me, how I was making everybody crack up as if playing an instrument virtuosically, their avid faces glued to me with awe and adulation, but also distrust and jealousy, if not unmasked villainy. When did it start? A friend's mother at the Christmas party, appreciating my routine, remarked to another mother: "Isn't he entertaining?" Then my mother's stepmother appraising my prospects in a steakhouse in Vermont: "Well he does have a Jewish nose." Then the premiere at the Majestic when the corpulent impresario announced with a tinge of malice: "Look at this young man. He'll go far." I took off into the moonlight after in Providence and passed right by Elliot Smith with the tattoos and the hoops in his earlobes, only a few years before he'd stab himself to death in the chest. "Your false self," a psychologist might say. So when did I lose it? (Did I?) When I moved to the city and holed myself up to write. I believed I was being honest. Being true to myself. But now after cancer I sometimes miss it. I catch myself wondering who I was and could be now.

Ativan

Now a pill; but in the hospital a needle's kiss: circulation, then a notion of milk leaking through blinds as my mind crept from bed toward my only sensible desire.

Save Oneself

One is of two minds: one doesn't want to go where one has been before but to discover someplace new; wishing with the same breath to regain one's health. The mountaintop school. Where one was taught to risk one's hand in her hand. Now one must guess: Did the old place sicken one with time? Will the old make one old again? Was it the strain of this incessant flight? speaking the mother tongue? observing? the exuding limbs and trunks and sandy strands? a table for one at the riverside free of every burden save oneself?

Passports

In my first I resembled a rugby player. American collegiate but really take your pick. A prick? Smirking cockily, lusty in love, my hair curling like a Roman legionnaire. Like Dürer but shorn and beardless; a preppy messiah. This was graduation weekend. Then a lifetime of vagabonding from Connemara to my next in California: bearded with beachy hair receding. Estranged, exiled to Wisconsin. Finally a victory before the fall. Still, we'd always have Provence . . . Yet somehow this afternoon I renew. I swivel my daughter upon the high stool: "Look there." I point. "We're going to another country," she explains to the photographer as the camera flashes.

Flying on Easter

There are similarities. You anticipate with dread, but also the promise of release. Waking early. Morning birds warble in the nightshade tree. Multitudes of nobodies. Where are we going? Where have we been? Many souls try your patience. An old woman accuses you of selfishness; you reflect, Is she wrong? You would like to describe how you're lost but surely she is too. You admire most, now, those who speak softly, say thank you.

Perseverance

LAX to Shannon then Kenmare by dinner and our ringleted daughter
bouncing downhill to the Sheen in a burnishing dusk. This is our reward
for surviving cancer, or a last-ditch effort to bank some memories of us
for her before it's too late. That our cottage abuts the "Old Cemetery"

I find a touch undermining. I am in between. And thereby put in mind of another dusk: Galway, January, 1997. Icy rain. I hung up the receiver inside the green box, wedged my pen in my journal, buttoned higher the olive-drab raincoat my mother had bought for me in the summer and ventured downtown—where was my umbrella? was I truly traveling without protection?—to a flat above an American-style diner not far from the Town Hall Theatre, where the Corrib capered over paisley stones beneath Wolfe Tone Bridge to the bay and the Arans beyond. The day before, I had toured a room in a house kitty-corner to Nora Barnacle's, but the children squalling in the schoolyard nearby posed an obstacle to art, I concluded. So tonight I would submit myself to an interview; "young professionals" was what they called themselves in the ad. They were cordial but reserved, almost as if they were baffled by me. When I rang them the next day from the green box in the rain they seemed to not know who I was. Had I lost my touch? "Right yeah," he said after she'd passed the phone along to him: the room was let. Was it was my goatee? my New York accent? my olive-drab raincoat dripping from the coat rack? Soon enough I'd find a bedroom in Salthill in a semidetached with a view from my small window of the ocean and Chemistry postgrads for housemates: "You Americans lack culture," they sought to educate me, "or a culture of your own, one you haven't stolen or fantasized. That's why you've come here." I tried to clear up their misunderstanding of America. We were both right. I heard them talking: "Could he be gay? I mean—a goatee? an olive-drab raincoat and poetry and plays?" "No, he's got to be straight, I've heard him listening to Tom Waits's *The Early Years* . . ." Why *hadn't* I brought an umbrella? The evening I learned I'd been turned down in Galway, I wandered through the deluge to an Italian restaurant and dumped myself upstairs by the fire to dry out. I drank a pint or three, inhaled a Bolognese, and recalled my Italian American Theatre professor who liked to pronounce perseverance as "per-severance," as if he were British though the Brits don't pronounce it that way, I don't think, and anyway he'd been born and bred in the Bronx. Once I overheard him referring to Bertolt Brecht as "Bresht." Another time in rehearsal he was running out of pointers for my acting and exploded: "Just be yourself, Dan! Do you even know how?"

French Press

I didn't know how so they showed me. This was the Huguenot Quarter and they were students at the nearby art school; they were working here for money, I presumed, to pay for paints, brushes, canvases. They pitied me. I'd speak only to order. Then scribbling my love letters. Reading eclectically in modern Irish poetry. Acclimatizing, convalescing; and all the while the fragrant first cup . . . second and third pouring gritty and charged with more tight-fingered mind-lightning. Because I was half-expecting (hoping?) I might someday find a family, I noticed a young mother breastfeeding in an aureole of sunlight through glass, shading her areola and her baby with an unfolded *Examiner*. I was at least vestigially Catholic, seduced by the votives the art students glided along the tables at the end of the day. They let me stay. I remember them now because I am newly in remission and coffee can be my only vice. (Some doctors say harmful, others say helpful.) Only one time do I recall becoming visible to them: climbing the steps to the balcony seating when I tripped and wiped out with my tray—glass shattered grounds scattered spreading brown on stone . . . They cleaned up before I could and brought me a new one without asking.

Evening Echo

Living in a city for the first time, or what looked like a city to me (stray dogs humping outside the barbershop amid clumps of hair eddying in the shadow of Shandon Steeple); since then I've forgotten how to feel forlorn. Instead I regret what time will take from me, but loneliness no longer moves me because time moves exponentially and I accept that any trip undertaken now will soon end. But back then a year in Ireland was like a suicide, and a birth: I had no choice but to try to make friends in the lobby after the show, carousing in smoky dank pubs, huddled together in the fluorescent chippery discussing literature passionately with the cold pomposity of youth. "You're very well read, aren't you?" a neglected Irish poet once remarked of me wryly. But most of the time I was alone. And as any pop-psych manual will tell you the brain is still branching, budding, fruiting at that age. What would have happened had I instead followed my primordial urge to become, let us speculate, an actor—would I have friends now, fame, money? Would I be healthy or have fallen ill sooner? I'll never know because this is when I grew inured to solitude. And almost to like it. Like those Sunday afternoons when I'd go out anxiously a-roving, the streets eerily deserted because the locals had all sequestered themselves inside with their kith and kin and every restaurant and pub was shuttered. In my mind's eye I can see in the dull sheen of a storefront's grimy glass the fluctuating reflection of my bent hungry frame, the pack looming on my back, the notebook inserted snugly in my coat pocket, and the way the setting sun splashes the window as if rebounding around corners in the lanes surrounding the art museum, diminishing with every turn. This is when I hear a boy of eleven or twelve calling—"*Evening Echo!*" He's hawking newspapers in the core of the city. Or he calls from the extremities somewhere along a thoroughfare like Saint Patrick's and his voice carries, his voice seeks me out. I don't know. I don't even know if newspapers were sold on a Sunday at twilight back then; likely I am conflating many memories of many twilights. But I hear again, as then, the cry of his repetition— "*Evening Echo . . . Evening Echo . . .*" Was this when I began to fall in love with myself? Or love's opposite?

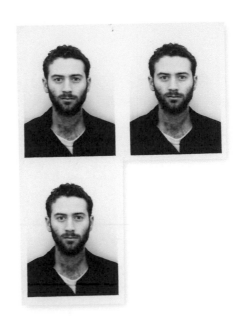

Life Will Be Harder

It must have been midnight in New Haven because dawn was breaking in Cork, where I'd been sleeping on the floor beside a defunct fireplace all winter. Rehearsing my hostage play. The bells of Saint Fin Barre's would wake me to the hiss of blood sausage and rashers but this morning the pay phone was ringing in the concrete stairwell. I had spurned him the year before; there would be no deferrals, he'd cautioned me then. And here he was calling to ask again: "Will you attend?" I felt flattered but conflicted. Already I knew I would travel alone, though decades would pass before I knew why. I told him so. My excuse was the cost and he could not believe his ears! "Life will be harder for you," he said and he hung up. I wasn't overly concerned. By life I assumed he meant only art.

The Parting Glass

Did I decide to stop drinking the moment the gastroenterologist said he'd encountered the tumor? I must have needed sedation to withstand the days (or weeks?) awaiting the diagnosis, then the weekend before my emergency surgery. But I can't for the life of me recall the last glass I raised to my lips, the way I don't remember the last time I was able to carry my daughter any distance in my arms. Or the last time I spoke with an old friend who's drifted away. When was my first? I didn't drink in school, save for some furtive slurping from tepid cans of cheap beer in the woods beside the parkway with my compadres. Or pissing dizzy in the oniony urinal of a thumping bar in the Caribbean. During college I was busy starving, delighting in my self-denial. It was in Ireland, unsurprisingly, nearly psychotic with the culture shock, after rehearsal as the director lined up pints across the tabletop, then staggering home to my hammock through the sea-slopping city beneath the buzzing streetlights, when I thought: *This is good company. This will pull me through.* Then the years in New York when I paid myself for writing with a ration of a single cold beer nightly. Then my family severed ties with me and I won't blame anybody but I can still hear the inveigling invitation to medicate my guilt. My unspeakable almost cellular sense of humiliation. Mainly I drank alone, deliberately: an unsociably happy hour or two of the auld black stuff, or brain-bleaching vodka, then wine during dinner. Then before, and after, the performance of something I'd written. I knew I was giving in. All the harm I have ever done, alas, I knew was to none but me. And I would run myself clean the next day Roman-Catholically. Deniably. Though lately I've begun to wonder if it was withdrawal when I spiked a fever of a hundred and four, vomiting black bile, a plastic tube shoved up my nose and snaked down my throat into my stomach, all the while perceiving the curious, lackadaisical souls in the doorway; the stampedes of souls tangling in the banks of the Styx; the hurricane of a terminus like Grand Central where one ghost paused as if to offer me directions. I haven't tasted a drop since the hospital anyway, save for a sip of wine I thought was water after reading a poem at the launch of a lit mag in a museum—I spat it back out. And felt chagrined, superstitious too: All my abstinence for naught! I'm not tempted anymore. Knowing myself, I suspect it was the night before the scalpel when I raised my glass in a final farewell and drank a health whate'er befalls, sorry for going away, wishing for one more day, bound for a new world, or bound for the gallows, gently rising and softly singing.

summer

They Look at You

They look at you as if to see. How have you changed? Has it aged you prematurely? they mean. Your skin hair weight. The sclera of your eyes. Is it hiding there somewhere inside you? Did I see you this morning jogging? Can I ask you, they ask you, what *kind* you had? They whisper, I was given a year and that was five years ago. Five years ago, they say, you'd be dead. They divulge, I had it; have it. Things are changing but we're vertical at least! My treatment makes me sleepy. My treatment makes me eat. My treatment leaves me incapable of honking my own horn. Some say nothing, at first. Cornered, in disguise: I have become a homebody. They smile. It has been too long, let's not let that happen again. Go, chase after your girl.

New Hampshire

Pursued by a blue pit bull leashed to a girl in floral rain boots crying no
Midnight no

New Hampshire 2

It was here in the summer I loved her for good: white asters at roadside, inchworms suspended from evergreens libidinously, the overhasty weddings of friends, her father over cocktails assailing my unsullied egoism. "What have you got against capitalism?" her mother pressed me at the country club. They threw us an engagement party in the barn where neighbors gathered, the first time they'd met my family who brought a Riesling from Virginia; my mother and my sister spoke solely to each other, while my father aggressively, as if defiantly, bullshitted with Boston bankers. Soon I would come clean: my family was a hoax and as such would not be attending the wedding. Then we stayed away for years, disgraced and industrious. And now this summer we return after our cancers, astonished and timorous. For her mother's seventieth she stands improvising a speech in the barn with the old neighbors, and when she's done I rise to enfold her feeling chastened, though I won't and don't let that stop me.

A Dryad

Correcting us our daughter shows the way and doesn't shrink but steps through columns of gargantuan rhododendrons, turns where two silver birch trunks twine, brushing firs and looping around the headless bust of a diplomat atop his hillock. We're waking up. She flies and we must let her go.

Alma Mater

The man who married us says he's read most of my books. Keeps them on his top shelf. But he's forgotten the story of my family: "Remind me: which one sued you?" His skin is suspicious, his hair like a dusting of snow on rust, though he's only lately emeritus. We move on. His wife has been riling our daughter; in front of everybody she asks me bluntly, "How is your health now?" And, "Do you still write?" We say goodbye and check into the B&B beside the town green. In the "Lincoln Room" at the top of the stairs we lower the shades but nobody rests. My wife has a migraine. We head out again. Our daughter wants to see the castle but she means the chapel where the carillon's been peeling. Students learning Arabic and Chinese conversing shyly in the grass. We process the crimson aisle. The empty pews smell sultry and holy. My wife cries behind her sunglasses. "Your father gave a speech here once," she tells our daughter, who pirouettes. I stumble outside into the shade of a tree planted twenty years ago for a classmate, a poet who drowned surfing in Costa Rica. We'd been planning to attend the concert on the green and spend the night in the Lincoln Room, but instead we decide to drive back to New Hampshire. On the way it rains but not much.

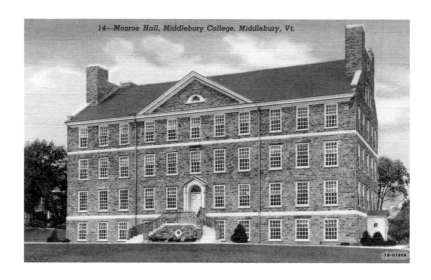

14—Monroe Hall, Middlebury College, Middlebury, Vt.

New Hampshire 3

At the engagement party my father must've been reminded of The Lake, as they had simply called it, or so I learned from his estranged brother because my father never mentioned it. The Lake was a Shangri-la owned by their Uncle Marv, and some weekends my father would drive across the Tappan Zee into Sullivan County, and every now and then he'd let his kid brother tag along. They'd stake their tent, hook worms and fish, hunt deer, and he was marvelous to be with—*Just marvelous,* his brother wrote me. *The only place I ever saw that kid, your father, absolutely at peace. Was there.* They were hoping their father would buy The Lake from Marv when Marv was old and selling, but their father couldn't swing it. He'd launched a plumbing supply store that quickly foundered. So somebody wealthy purchased The Lake and essentially this taught my father a lesson. He was done with school and working for his father by then, and it embarrassed him, the whole Irish Plumber thing. And without The Lake he lost interest in staking tents, hooking worms and fish. The hunt. He lost interest in his brother. He married my mother. And with her family money set out to establish himself as a successful corporation of one—computers, white-collar, self-made— and failed. And managed on his wife's funds, feigning work. His kids could scarcely stand him and he didn't seem to care. So when he met my fiancée's father for the first time at that party, a corporate executive with a shock of salt-and-pepper hair, lake-adjacent property and prestige cars, cigars, friends and affectionate progeny—it's obvious why my father, and with him the rest of my family, refused to attend our wedding here the next year. There were other reasons, of course, but this is one of the more sympathetic explanations I have had cause to imagine.

In Time for the Lesson

Told myself I would and thanks be did by the end of our visit make it once around the lake past old friends' windows sick now flown breast deep in consequential incarnations the alpaca corral the mossed chapel the exhausted slipway faltering midway at the colonial boneyard before burning in my dogged rise then lurching stiffly down past the marsh-like pond to tie the knot of my start-and-stop at the shoreline as my girl paddles in the putty-soft shallows learning how to swim

Napping after Cancer

feels dangerous, and almost nothing like traveling to Saint-Rémy when my wife was expecting and beginning to show, her morning sickness lifting, to pass through Roman arches and chrome-yellow wheat fields beneath desiccated cypresses lining trails pocked with irises and blue mulberries where van Gogh painted through barred windows (omitting said bars), and eschewing the guided tour we indulged ourselves instead in the market square gorging on cheeses so slender the two of us even her despite her bulge; then zigzagging downhill into the grand allées between colonnades of sighing plane trees stretching in the straightaway across for the intimation murmuring from her body to mine: our child tumble-turning inside. How could we know what was waiting for us just around the bend? In the afternoon we pulled over to rest our eyes drowsy from the drive in a gravelly rest stop, shoulder to shoulder like effigies with our seats reclined and the windows wide, dandelions unfurling in a breeze.

Forgiveness

A cannonade of Santa Ana and flashing back it's when I was dazzled by the dislocation: outside for the first time since surgery and my near-death intubation, balanced upon the edge of a concrete bench in nothing but a paper gown, in the heat of the desert, eavesdropping on a hundred healthy humans eating. On the patio of the cantina. Doctors and nurses, staff and visitors. Laughter, chitchat, gossip. Plans for the weekend. Some must have been the loved ones of the sick and dying but they were all the same to me: free to go, frivolous; nobody noticing. The needles in my arms, hands, spine, my bulbously overloaded, teetering IV tree chirping. I was doing everything I could to endure. Massaging my thigh as if to reform the clay. Why wouldn't they see? Incrementally I may be learning to forgive.

The Crab

Like the summer after my brother tried suicide, when nothing was resolved or named, and the seaweed-streaming shoals of the bay teemed with cancer the crab in mutating proliferation, sideways scuttling and anything not palpably sand became envisioned chitin in my mind and launched me scrambling into my dubious craft. This is how I live now in remission, bobbing along peering past my reflection at the bottom of a rising tide.

Worry

A grain of sand under the skin. A pearl I wished to pluck. Inexorably accruing in the heel of my foot. At night irresistibly I would dig into it with a pin burned brilliant in the stovetop's range. It bled, it healed; inexorably it grew. The doctor numbed it, framed it in paper, sliced and scooped it out. A planter's wart, I thought he said. Like a seed. See the nervy roots? Then back to school. Where I'd peel my sock to show the bandage with pride. Though inwardly I feared its return. Worry, my mother said, caused it. Which is what she said about my other fears: of germs, of abduction, of possession, all of which was a kind of code for my brother's body dangling in a noose, for my brother's wrists slashed in a bathtub filled with blood, for my brother's mouth around our father's gun. Head gone. The more you worry about it the more you make it occur, my mother said. Better to forget it, if you know what's good for you. But I didn't. In hidden ways I've treasured it, writing it over and over again. Inexorably. And it never did come back, or hasn't yet.

On Time

O how did we say in our youth O that was so long ago O anyhow now ten years are as three as two as

Prometheus

I was already bleeding when flying to Heathrow then Edinburgh then hazarding the wee roads to St Andrews where I received the message I'd been shortlisted for a prize. For delivering the fire of faraway wars to a theatre in Notting Hill. Inside a shoebox up the staircase from reception, on a single bed beneath a headstone of a window, bathroom in the hall: foreign poets came and went below. I did not participate adequately. I shared a podium with a minister. The audience faced us comatose; Presbyterian, I supposed. A lyrical shepherd, sick now, or so I've heard, flashed his flask but I declined. I walked the West Sands alone. I christened a new journal with a new pen. I recognized a war poet, whose wife has since died of breast, to whom I should have introduced myself; I met an American poet, who would go on to blurb my book before he passed away of lung. We both heard we'd been snubbed by an influential editor, but I was too tired to care—from colon and liver, I would soon learn. I slept too much. And woke to seagulls like eagles crying, confused: would I live or die?

Fragment

The open parenthesis of birth

On Symbols

I wore it every day during chemotherapy, while I balded surreptitiously, plasticky filaments accumulating in the plastic mesh of a baseball cap emblazoned with the silhouette of a Trojan. USC. My wife's coworker had survived stage 4 throat and wanted me to have it. I couldn't wear bandannas—too on the nose, and foreboding. I believed: *This cap is pure white like a bandage, marked with the red promise of the medicinal toxins galloping through my veins.* After treatment I threw my cap away because it had served its purpose, but also because it reminded me of suffering and felt like bad luck now.

Now

Everybody has cancer, everybody has had cancer, everybody will survive. Everybody will die of it; or something. Everybody requires consolation or advice, guidance or silence. It's common. A bald mother is swinging her girl in the park. An old woman with waxen chemo skin plays with her salad alone. A bottle of urine in the gutter reminds me but I don't despair. There may be another half. Another forty years or more. Must I get a real job now? Must I become bored again? Meanwhile the forever war drags on.

New Journal

O that I may live to see these pages yellow

Whether

My wife's concern is cancer recurring: I'm more likely. I deny it and here we go again. A tempered romance should be otherwise; otherwise what has been the point? I keep my secret from her: *Another pubescence is stirring.* Crows are dispersing, repair trucks reversing: everyday omens of an unthinkable future. The wind is bombastic and fronds could kill but the rainstorm as we ramble is approaching music.

Genetics

The hidden staircase, outdoors and so steep it's almost a ladder shortcutting between intestinal hillside lanes, is deceptively treacherous where the cement's unstable. Here and there. Chips and shards. Hollow divots. Scabs and scars. Worn by footsteps and wind and rain that scours the canyons in our flashing winters. Why the crack in this step and not in that? Why the foothold lost here and not there? Surely the designer is to blame, or the maker. Or our place in time. Or the fault unknown unsettling. There is no rail. We descend with our hands open.

Aliens

Some day we will die? My mother unfastened her eyes and sighed yes someday, naturally, everybody . . . Frequently I found myself wishing our father would keel over, thus liberating us all from his bullying ubiquity. He seemed old, though he wasn't yet forty. This was the same conversation in which I asked my mother if she and Father were who they claimed to be. I'd seen Ray Bradbury's *Martian Chronicles* on TV and felt unmoored by one particular chronicle in which an astronaut lands in Green Bluff, Illinois. Clapboard houses, church spires, wind pumps and cornstalks. I'll be damned! he cries. It doesn't make sense because he's been bound for Mars for months on a space cruiser called the Zeus II, if I'm not mistaken, with some other crewmen, I think, though for convenience's sake I'm leaving them out; and here he is enjoying a Sunday dinner with his family. All of whom have been dead for years now. Yet miraculously they're alive again: parents and sibling revelry, fried chicken and pie. That night as his mother tucks him tightly in his boyhood bed, sitting beside his feet, singing a lullaby, her eyes enkindle like evening stars; and it dawns on our hero that this is indeed the Red Planet, and it's all been a dream, a snare that was baited with his nostalgia and his need, and his deceased mother is in reality a shapeshifting alien who, along with the rest of his false family, their eyes glowing in the darkness like constellations, like the cosmos, encompass the astronaut and tear his mortal vessel apart. The moral of the story being: You're on your own here, kid.

Voices in the Prep Room, Beverly Hills

Birth year? 1935. '43. White Plains; above the Bronx. The BQE to White Castle: jogging 'cross the Brooklyn Bridge. Nadine. I said to her, Go to an eatery! Why wait for me? My name is Mr. Meeks. Aortic aneurysm. Cancer? Oh sure. Skin caught before the heart. Gloria's only a friend. I don't have much family left. I'm tough. You know I was born for this.

A Nurse's Tattoo

The butterfly's wings are lungs. The chemo chair's a chair. The needle slides into my vein and I slide into the segmenting orifice; then holding my breath. *Breathe*, the machine intones. And repeat. I tear the tape away, toss it in the trash at the intersection. A glimmer of an inkling of what I mustn't say, or know. Waiting gladly for the light. The bruising will deepen, then fade.

The Prize

These CT scans are a lot like exams at school, at which I did quite well without ever excelling like my brother, the suicidal one, who thrived inside the confines of a puzzle. But these tests are existential; the waiting is the game. While faceless readers interrogate the entrails of my living body-at-work. Not unlike the contest of a career in the arts either—substantiation meant to refute myself. In Tennessee I'd visit my mailbox at the end of the driveway morning, noon, and night. And without fail the empty mouth. Yet sometimes after drought: a check. I'm desperate for their decision now; it has happened before. Like a winter morning walking the dog in a numinous mist when a strange voice in my ear exclaimed—"You've won!"

Lazarus in Remission

Is he a poet? Does he just pick up the pen again? Let us imagine he lives contentedly and not weirdly at all with his spinster sisters. Can he go back to having sex? Can any woman bear the touch of where he's been? Or does he always look a little off, what with his earthen skin and his beard of white lichens? Does he stink? Does he lie awake in bed wondering if the procedure is incomplete, if swaddling bands trail from his feet, if centipedes ribbon his fingers and his toes? Will he ever be a man again? Will he rage bellow weep craving alcohol sugar bloody meat? Before and after everything, he knows he has been saved. So the world at least looks new; he likes life more. Which is probably when and why he drops out of the picture.

Why Write

Returning to the conference after chaos—the last time I was here was maybe a month before my wife found her lump; six months more and they'd cut me open too—I am transported to another summer when, on the convocational evening like the first morning of school, shy greetings in the heat beside the bus from the airport in line for dinner—Who will sit with me? Who will read my words? Who will help mollify the tyranny of my self-scrutiny?—I saw a woman crying. Like a child dazed glancing helplessly escorted by the elbow from the boisterous dining hall by the conference director whose face remained firmly placid like a kindly pediatrician. I asked what was wrong and somebody said her husband had dropped her off in the afternoon and, arriving home, dropped dead of an embolism. She was in shock. Understandably uncomprehending. "I can't go now"—desperate to convince anybody who'd listen—"I have to stay. I have to find a way to put this all down on paper."

South

A body is turning in the woods a hawk is hovering above a bedroom
yawns with mold

B—

The first time I saw him was after he'd survived. This was meant to be
a lecture, but there he was sitting sidelong in a chair beside the lectern
describing how Christ appeared at his bedside in the hospital after
surgery for the kind of cancer I would have one day too. The sunlight
hit him evangelically. I was still lightheaded from the laughing gas, half-
numb and -dumb and -slobbering after the placement of a dental crown
earlier that morning. "You know, there's a tradition of good writers
with bad teeth," R— would buck me up later that day, before launching
into another disquisition about sentimentality on the porch of the inn
where the faculty were staying. All week long I'd been contemplating

jettisoning everything for a short-haired older woman (she was nearly thirty). But that morning watching B— I felt shaken, then embarrassed for him, then embarrassed for some reason for myself and for all of us in attendance. Then two years pass and he's flown over the mountains in W—'s light airship to perform a reading in an almost Elizabethan oak-paneled hall, dreary with suits of armor and reproachful paintings of Episcopalians in Oxbridge-style gowns, where he rhapsodized about writing, "the party at the keyboard"—*There is no other reason*, he seemed to be pleading. At the reception we shook hands briefly and I said something awkwardly complimentary; he smiled uneasily, greasily as if I were a liar. He died of a heart attack not long after. I'm glad in the end he went quick.

I.M. M.P.

He called to me from atop a tree: barefoot, in dungarees, with a sprig of weed in his smile and a satyr's beard. This was Bread Loaf in the '90s and we were roommates. We'd been friendly enough in college but he was a townie who worshipped Beat poetry (his aunt knew Ginsberg, he liked to remind me) while I aspired to be the Gabriel García Márquez of Westchester County. Late one night he kissed an au pair in the woods while I lay in bed with *One Hundred Years of Solitude*. More years passed and I kept tabs on him. Protesting, he leapt into the East River to elude the cops. While I locked myself in black boxes. He motorcycled across the Hindu Kush. I was envious. In my annus mirabilis he died, seeking the source of the Nile when a heatstroke took him. While I limped along the groaning strand in Aldeburgh, a belletrist with the worm already twisting in my gut. We both had been roses. Why have I waited so long to mend my ways?

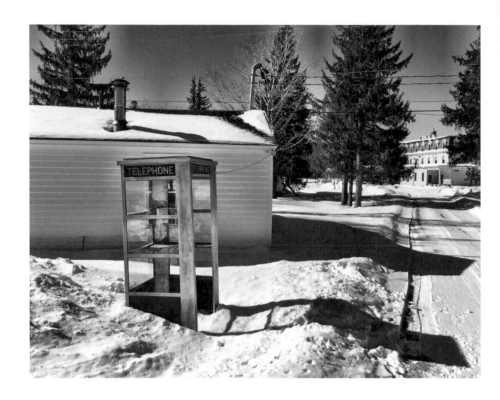

Unpublished

A middle-aged poet (who has recently died of cancer) gave an old poet (somehow still here) a manuscript. This first poet was rumored to have shot a lover in her youth—a poet too; down south. But in grad school whenever I saw her she was typically smoking and edgy and not noticing me. I lived in the old poet's house, minding his bills and water pipes, while he and his wife, another poet, sabbaticalled in Paris. Every wall in every room was lined with shelves crammed with books; the effect was positively pathological. I read and slept in the old poet's study where his atheist wife, a German-born survivor of the Third Reich, required that he keep his books on religion, the occult, but also books bordering on faith like philosophy and psychology (the old poet's family were snake handlers, or something, in Kansas in the '30s). One day when I was having trouble writing I found a box beneath his desk containing this younger, Southern poet's manuscript, beginning with a handwritten page (I don't remember the title) in purple ink and adorned with a doodled cartoon heart. Love poems. "I don't know if these are any good," she'd scrawled. "Maybe you'll tell me?" I could not believe that famous poets, as I thought of them, could not know. I pondered who these poems were for. She was married to a handsome poet. I read the poems and felt guilty. So I placed the lid back on the box, the box back under the desk, and raced out of doors. Famished. I wanted to eat in a restaurant, wanted to make love. I have no idea if that manuscript ever saw the light of day.

Elizabeth

Are you near Elizabeth not yet you reply equivocally but I will take it from your perspective a day may be as the thirty years that have passed since I pilfered from your deathbed a thread of your unraveling mind like breath and breathed: *You are my true mother.* That restless summer you lay wasting I was already writing in my mind while outside running realising I could delay I could chronically cure you with a word a turn of phrase then coiling around to worry and rework this troublesome delusion of fixing

Secondhand

Toiling for atonement, in those early days I worked through the night at an investment bank; my comrades were actors and playwrights, poets and singers and our harried boss, we'd soon learn, had a blood cancer and wouldn't survive the winter. Rising muddled at noon I would retire to the second room in my sublet with the bricks and the crumbling mortar, boxes of photos of the leaseholder and her faded friends with feathered hair, skinny-dipping upstate before AIDS; and I would write or gaze instead through my window on a courtyard where the snow accumulated on trash cans, audience to an old woman across the way ironing in her underwear. Bohemia, at last! My walls were decorated with Javanese shadow puppets, marionettes, gargoyles. The furniture was at least secondhand. So-called water bugs would beach themselves on the threadbare rug during downpours. The toilet was off the kitchen, no shower but a clawfoot tub with a hose and a wide-mouthed pitcher for rinsing. I didn't cook. Voices passing my door were customers tramping up- and downstairs from the gnomish, long-bearded dealer above me. The super was long bearded too; he lived in the basement with a woman and several (it was unclear how many) long-bearded men with fanatical eyes—every one of them allegedly members of a sex cult with a "queen bee" structure, whatever that meant exactly. The super commandeered my new down coat when it was delivered and left beside the mailboxes. He'd smile at me teasingly, but I was too scared to ask. Often I'd see him cozy in my coat as he hauled the trash from the courtyard to the sidewalk, as I tiptoed from my apartment to run the gauntlet of shoppers to the charity dive and its hoard of used books, underlined, annotated, dedicated in the hands of the dead. The prices were penciled faintly inside. I read more books there than I could ever hope to buy.

I Used to Get So Nervous

The infant with leukemia is married now. I am told. A mother my age and approximately my diagnosis has been informed of a spot that is "fixable." They tell her. (She calls it "maintenance.") My girl stands barefoot in the wet grass, speaking to me on the phone, when lightning splits a neighbor's tree. A tick is found nestled in my wife's calf. I deliver my new lecture; the response is uncertain. As it ought to be. Long days, the angel told me. Go tell Pharaoh.

Headshots

When I had them done in San Francisco I sensed both life and death converging. A whitewashed studio—walls, floor, ceiling; a tidal wave of windows. The photographer was a wiry redhead armored in sleeves of tattoos. Pendulous gauges. His thing was to take a series of wet-plates as if you'd survived Antietam. He'd been doing this with PTSD war vets and that's how I heard of him—not that I'd ever seen combat, and yet stupidly I felt somewhat qualified. He said: "I'll shoot a few in color— for commercial use." Then he let the light into the box, imprisoning these iterating ghosts of myself in slivers of glass; captured, as if this were me now forever: book jackets and obituaries, etc. He telegraphed the shutter on his digital camera: and instantly somebody else was there, somebody who wasn't. That desecrated soldier I had written about without his consent? My mother's damning at a distance? In retrospect I look bleary, bloated; my beard's too bushy. At the time I told myself I was solidifying with age; my wife was substantially pregnant and dads should have some weight to throw around. Do I look healthier than I do today? Or was I already harboring the cancer? Secretly I half expected the laurel wreath and plaudits, oratory in the rotunda—that sort of classical sequence. Not so many years earlier on Chestnut St. in winter in Princeton I went through my Graham Greene phase, his books but also his life: the amphetamines, the appropriately green baize door separating his home from the school where his father taught and where he got bullied. And that day in San Francisco I was remembering how Greene liked to say he could always tell when good fortune was heading his way, in terms of reviews and awards and sales; it's uncontrollable, of course—luck builds like the weather and breaks in your favor sometimes; rains on you too. This is what I'm thinking in my headshots: Something's coming, a reckoning, a settling of debts, maybe even my comeuppance. My gaze is in fact frightened. Because all this happened and more.

Use

We used to clean ourselves. Then we hired two women who claimed to be sisters, though one was loquacious and flirtatious while the other sister wasn't. From a country where as children they witnessed beheadings funded in part by our parents' taxes. They left us soon after my wife's surgery—all the pill bottles and stained bandages in the trash and we understood: they hadn't signed on for this. We found another cleaner when I got sick. She was quiet, and she worked so thoroughly that our things could be hard to find. She'd restore our pill-bottle caps to our pill bottles, ordering and stacking them away as if we no longer needed them. Which funnily enough has me thinking of the urologist with the urine-colored hair, who reminded me testily of my late stage, after I'd insisted on twilight sedation before I would permit him to poke around inside my bladder to extract some necrosis and sew me up properly this time. My wife stormed out, a rogue wave. The urologist would rather be surfing, and had other patients besides. An older nurse confided that her daughter, born coincidentally the same year as me, she said, had cancer, a rare form in her case and "Look she's still alive!" This was when I broke down, something I'd never done with a stranger before, and she rocked me shushing from side to side. We clean house ourselves now. Again. Thanks to them (and so many others) I sit here at my desk, working, such as it is, trying in my mostly self-serving way to be of use.

Pride

The concern fell dormant the whole time I was surviving, cowed, tamed by the tragedy. I am more than annoyed by its resurgence, this gnawing at the bars. I am ashamed as I am awed by the creature desiring to be wild again. But remember: the righteous shall be bolder than a cancer, sayeth the updated proverb, like lions pacing in our cells. The future contains and uncages itself.

Reminder

The play goes unreviewed. So far. You promised not to read them but how then are you supposed to know if anybody gives a damn? Critics, clicking their pens against their notepads in the watery light reflecting from the stage, are dumbstruck with disappointment; or their pity for your condition is stronger than their revulsion for your theatrical catastrophe. Maybe you have been spared; maybe it's true that nobody is really watching but you.

After Borges

There is another me who wrote plays I have neither seen nor read. Once I received a rejection meant for him; the works in question, if I recall correctly, were *Frantic!* and *City Banker*. People don't like to be mistaken for other people. Except one time when I was an interloping neophyte at Bread Loaf in the '90s, lounging in an Adirondack chair in a meadow of freshly mown hay, and a slightly older woman asked me, Are you *the*

Dan O'Brien? And I answered Yes without thinking because it felt nice; we soon cleared things up. She had been referring to the buffalo rancher with alopecia whose books I have since read. He's good. He's quite popular in France. We shared the same agent for a New York minute but she wanted me to write like him, or because mine was a memoir she wished my life was like his—maybe not so much buffalos but bees. "Have you considered beekeeping?" she queried. There's the comedy writer with my name; the biracial American decathlete who struck gold in Atlanta; a bearded West End Dan O'Brien who's treading the boards currently in *Mamma Mia!* (And these are only the D. O'Bs I know of—Googling myself is mortifying; maybe this explains the beards?) I know personally a bearded TV actor who erroneously receives my royalties from time to time. He hands me the check when we get coffee. He lives on Sunset now. His wife's a playwright but for a long while, at least according to IMDB, this Dan O'Brien was married to my wife. In a play once he played me; it was a play I wrote and I played me too, two sides of me wrestling. Psychologically. We look similar, though he's a bit bigger. Which reminds me—don't ever tell anybody that they resemble anybody else. Just don't do it! Especially if you're tempted. I was giving a reading as a grad student in Providence, bescarved and inflamed and fizzling after, when a slightly older couple approached: Do you happen to know X in Iowa? Or was it East Anglia. I did not. Sadly they shook their heads. You look so much like him—tatterdemalion-chic: the same thrift-shop peacoat, same thrift-shop bald-kneed wide-wale corduroys, gaunt sharp hips severely belted, fair of face and bravely bearded. You are the spitting image of our friend, they declared. Him before he forgot who he was. You are his avatar, the woman whispered. I thanked them and raced home to my *OED* (remember the *OED*?) and after perusing the definition I had no idea what they meant, or what it was they truly wanted. This was before the movie. At least X had a name and not this everyman appellation I've been working with. My parents did their best to name all six of their children almost anonymously. To protect us from teasing, they reasoned. From any insult that they were not personally providing themselves. So I knew it would be my lifelong task to distinguish myself. To make myself noteworthy. Which is foolhardy and reminds me of that first Dan O'Brien, the playwright—I had meant to say this at the start: he went on a blind date once with a playwright who'd later become my friend, though I've lost touch with her, I don't know why honestly, maybe because she's more successful than me and writes TV crime procedurals now; or maybe there's another reason? because looking back I wonder if she stoked the tiniest flickering interest in me when I was somebody else, somebody striving desperately to be who he wasn't. Anyway she told me this Dan O'Brien lost her while mansplaining his oeuvre to her, prizing open another steamed mussel, decanting a flowery sauvignon blanc: "But I don't write anymore. Why should I even try? Dan O'Brien's already said everything Dan O'Brien needs to say."

Dedication

What do you do when an old friend has dedicated his poem to you because he thought you were dying? As you are—we all are; who knows the day or hour? A particle of clot, a red light sailed through and lights out, show's over. Nobody had warned me. I bought his new collection because I like him, and turning the page I am shocked then touched then unnerved. The sense of a sentencing. My name in stone. He's my age, give or take. With a wife and a daughter and a grizzling beard like mine. I think the poem is strong. Ekphrastic, that is, a poem about a painting I'm unfamiliar with. Maybe my name was appended as an afterthought, a why-not, a coup de grâce unintentionally? But its closing lines evoke the doom-dim afternoons of the languishing months in the bardo of chemotherapy. The static nebulas vibrating in the cobwebbed corner above my sickbed. He has conjured that perfectly. So I must remember to write and thank him.

fall

Past

Often we'd pass each other in our childless years, the two of us running our daily routes through the neighborhood. She was tiny, with a billowy veil of frizz. Did she notice me too? And why was she free in the middle of the day? Was she an artist like me? I worried she was anorexic or exercise-bulimic, at least. Saddled with a chauvinist for a husband or something worse. She was pregnant when my wife was. Later we'd pass each other frazzled, pushing our bawling strollers; if we paused to talk I feared we would kiss. Then my wife's diagnosis—there was no time to waste. They harvested her eggs the day after her surgery. I drove her at dawn from the hospital to the clinic and a doctor who appeared regularly on a reality TV show. My wife was sedated but still flinching, furiously cursing when I took a turn sharply, or hit a bump or a pothole. An oxygen tank clanked in the back seat (in case she had trouble with her breathing). My cramping was racking; I was unwittingly closing in on my own diagnosis. An attractive, yawning young nurse ushered me into a brightly lit closet with a wipeable recliner and a flat-screen (cycling through soft-focused photos of fountains and flowers) where she told me to "use the plastic cup." Five or six eggs were fertilized but nothing took. Then I was wiped clean too. During my chemotherapy I'd sometimes shamble past that neighborhood woman with her new baby, the first one toddling. And just this arsenic hour as I trudge along in my remission, my pending cure, I behold: she has begotten a third. One marches, one skips, one tosses a teething toy over the lip of the well-used stroller. We pass on the sidewalk outside a watering hole that's roaring like a rapids.

Shared Wall

Our neighbor's doing well a year after her treatment. She was diagnosed a year after my diagnosis. We had told her about it in the driveway and she cracked a weird kind of joke: "Stay away from me!" As if I were contagious. I stood smiling, speechless. When we first met I was wary, as is my way. I thought she was crazy because she had been calling through our mail slot all morning, "Hello? Hello?" I chose to ignore her; I was busy writing (I'd soon find out she was a writer too, but for TV). Then an hour or so later I'm walking the dog and she ambushes me beneath a banana tree, and I have no choice but to proffer my polite introduction, and she asks if her house is haunted because she hears like this knocking from her stairs? but nobody's ever there? and this morning she'd fled from the house and even called through my mail slot ha ha ha and only now does she feel safe enough to come home. I calm her down, as is my way also, explaining how there's really nothing to worry about, it's just the house, our houses and this thin wall we share and sometimes I can't tell either if somebody's tromping up or down our stairs or hers on the other side. "Don't be scared," I say. "The ghosts we're hearing are probably each other."

Disaster 2

Even celebrities get cancer. She's diagnosed the week of her winning her umpteenth Emmy. I'm on my way to her house along streets named for Seven Sister Ivies like Bryn Mawr, Barnard, Radcliffe, Mount Holyoke . . . A sighting of a Rolls. Vistas from the palisades of contrails etching the blue vault of the bay. Everybody's the same. Soccer moms, fiscally astute fathers. Notes nailed to trees: No dogshit, Don't filch our lemons, Don't disturb the occupants. I feel safe here. Despite who I am and where I'm from. The TV star says her treatment is like swimming in a pool and she must keep her eyes at all times trained on the ladder toward which she strokes. Because there is a shark in the pool with her, which is unlikely, but accurate because cancer feels like that: the shark in the pool of your own blood. She keeps her secret, for now. I step lightly up to her door (remarkably close to the curb; no gate) and leave a tote bag of my wife's chemo survival supplies, as they are becoming closer friends now.

Forever for Sale

I presumed it was cursed. This leprous slantwise ranch on the corner capped with the green weather vane of a greyhound. I never saw a soul come or go. The windows leered. Regardless I would daydream, Maybe we can afford it? And today I can't find it. Are we free? Has it been repainted? No—gone, razed in a day.

Labor Day

The heat breaks late. Burbank's still burning. NoCal in the hundreds. Texas is flooding. Chilly in New York and London. I run on the beach and feel strong—in my gait, my thighs—like a teen. Feel my nerves reconnecting, scars itching and fading. Hairline recovering. My middle thickening. I ogle the gem-colored aisles and aisles of alcohol. As in, Can't we try again? As I pull into the fish market the car in front brakes for some geriatric and I think, Great, now I've become involved in this poor guy's fugue state, his dementia, his cancer, whatever because he's inching along . . . Blocking traffic. He's accompanied and I recognize them as our former landlords. Methuselean and meddlesome because they used to live beside us; they munched their muesli on a patio outside our bedroom window. His sister in Sweden was slowly dying of bone or lung cancer, I forget which. He was skeletal even then, especially when weeding the yard shirtless, but he jogged or speed-walked really in flimsy short-shorts like a pioneering health-nut, as he'd been running since the '70s to and from his lab along San Vicente, six miles each way to UCLA. He was a molecular biologist, I believe. His wife was a non-practicing child psychologist and unreformed New York Jewish communist. Their children lived out of state. They'd invite us down for dinner, and dragging our feet we'd go and get fed something rich and warmed-over and drink lots of wine while they bickered about Freud the charlatan and the hysteria surrounding monosodium glutamate. We were captive; we were courteous. Also they liked to (unconsciously?) orchestrate arguments between tenants about noise and would address a stopped up toilet with alacrity but do a crappy job; the whole place was held together by patchwork and deceit. I grew to dislike them. And here they are in the parking lot, alive if not exactly kicking. Sun setting behind them. The first cool breezes of our precipitous fall. Leaving as I arrive. He's pushing a walker on wheels; she looks about the same. She seems to recognize me as I reverse and drive away.

Success

Not long ago, just before and after the baby, there were these moments when we thought it could happen. We had clambered out of the crater of our ambition, though we claimed—and believed—we didn't want fame. Some fortune maybe, a house with grass, a college fund. Things that accrue, not decay. Not a drip inside the walls, then the flood. Now every second's unexpected. I do not wish to achieve anything any longer or not for the old reasons. I wish only to wake beside my wife as if nothing is always changing. I wish only to know our only daughter when she has changed uneventfully into a woman.

Therapists

The first one cried for me as I embarked upon the retelling of my congenital complaints. Or was she sniffling for herself? remembering her first hurt—what had sat her there in that dark office. Was she crying for her life: divorce? death? I was nineteen and bone dry. So I never went back. The next one was, perhaps for good reason, a decade later and she told me she dreamed of me. We were riding a tandem bicycle and I was having trouble pedaling and wouldn't let her help me and wasn't that revealing? I never once withdrew a single tissue from her well-positioned tissue box. In the dark office with the barred windows near Washington Square, her desk and coffee table crowded with books about S&M and nymphomania. Because I did not see with my own eyes my brother leaping from the attic window, she asked if it was possible it never happened? Maybe I misunderstood? She suspected my mother had poisoned our dogs. She saw a play of mine and in the lobby after seemed pleasantly disappointed. Then after my parents disowned me she assured me that I would feel less obliterated, eventually, in say oh five to ten years. The next one helped; the dark office across Broadway from the Ed Sullivan Theater was sparsely furnished. Her specialty was anxiety, with skills honed at Bellevue. She was the first to speak plainly: "Your parents did not love you." She looked unwell, almost translucent. I'd joke with myself: Is she a ghost? Will I turn up next week to find her dark office empty? "It's been empty since 1997," a janitor tells me, pushing his broom down the hall . . . Things speed up; I was moving around. A hippie in a long velvet gown in Wisconsin in a brown building like a bank. In Beverly Hills a Tasmanian having an affair, I was certain, with my wife's therapist, a surly German. Another I don't remember save for the mirrored high-rise where we'd meet; all I could think about was earthquakes. The one who told me we were headed for a global plague and I laughed it off. Then the one I referred to as "Dr. Hands," behind her back, of course, because when I would talk, which was most of every session, as it should be, she would stare at my hands. Alarmed, as if they were dripping with blood. I hypothesized she was researching a paper about "the camouflage of gesticulation," or something like that, and I did begin to notice how habitually I was gesticulating to one side or the other as if pushing, arranging, isolating all of my psychic baggage in the crawl space of my mind. I tried not to move. I meant to ask her what she saw in my hands, but I never got around to it. I was seeing her when my wife was undergoing chemotherapy. When I mentioned that I had symptoms too, she advised me to call a doctor, but I procrastinated and by the time I was diagnosed with my own cancer I was too ashamed to call her again. Now, I'll agree there is an elephant in the dark office: so few of my therapists have been men. The truth is I distrust them, though I have tried. One asked me if my father had had any dreams and I'd no idea, and didn't care, and he went on and on about his thwarted aspiration to be a jazz singer. He wore Rollerblades in the dark office and grumbled about his wife. When I stopped calling he wrote a letter saying he hoped I wasn't leaving therapy altogether, because it was clear I was sick. I never cried for any of them. I guess I'm reflexively trying to make the listener cry. The reader. Today is for drugs; a psychiatrist around my age. Who overresponds, as if making fun of me, could be sarcastically. She's uneasy. Maybe nervous that what has afflicted me could afflict her too? Has it already? She's angular and ashen. Fragile-faced, exhausted. Saintly yet skeptical: she wants me to make certain I'm not denying myself the "occasional joy" (her words). She fills out my prescription, prints the invoice for insurance—eighty-five minutes will run me five hundred dollars—and as she moves from chair to desk I see the palsy in her leg. MS? ALS? Or something she was born with? Her smartphone case is bubblegum pink so I think of her kids and a life she wisely keeps hidden.

Anger

This prospective therapist is a Vietnam vet, I've been told. He texted the wrong address; the address he texted does not exist. I see him exit the public restroom. We wetly shake. He reminds me of a sickly owl. Military patches on his leather bomber, an old Navajo rug in his office where he asks if I'm aware that OCD is anger unspoken and right away I'm angry. He notes this. "How does that make you feel, what I said?" Instead I say coolly, "I'm concerned you might be too old-fashioned." He shrugs. "It's what I believe." He would like to seem humble and humanistic. But he's condescendingly uncomplicated. He warns me that we will need to be a team, he and I. He's had another melanoma removed recently, and on the way out walking me toward the elevator he says he's been diagnosed with prostate. Just the other day. "They caught it early." And now I'm the one counseling him: "It happens to everybody eventually." I won't be back. He asks me to let him know what I decide because otherwise "I'll be thinking about you," and I think that's at least part of the problem here. Like the Russian acupuncturist who told me, weeks after my first surgery, that my cancer was likely caused by "holding onto anger." How angry I was at her for saying that! How angry I am at those who think they know; who are in truth afraid. My father the last time I saw him, shouting in the brutal sun: *You have a problem with anger!*

The Chair

My room overlooked the chapel. Pigeons nested in my dormer window. I had such lofty intentions. I even attempted a novel in there; the walls vibrated with my manias. One night after another agonizing phone call with my girlfriend in Philadelphia—I was trying to break up with her without feeling cruel; I felt stymied—I hung up and stood up and kicked the wooden chair on its side like a hanging, stomped it until it splintered and the leg cracked clean away. I felt satisfied, then terrified as I sneaked the wreckage of my love past the closed doors of my friends asleep or engaged in percussive sex, and into our common room. Where nobody was around. And left it behind. It wasn't mine. The school had so many chairs who'd notice? But a security guard let himself into every room to check. My phone rang. Did you dump your broken chair? I confessed I had. How could I explain? The voice on the line didn't care, so long as I paid up.

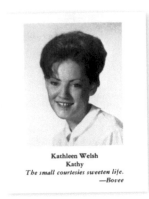

Bikes

Was it a doctor's idea? To counteract the disconcerting, incipient flab of their twenties? Four children (so far) and her figure going. As for him he'd been growing steadily, hunkered there in the entropy of his study like a bear at the zoo. Or was exercise prescribed to remedy their sanity: their repressed depressions, their carousel of paranoias, the folie à deux that wed them? My father's fear of flying and failure? The chilling hand of my mother's institutionalized brother forever fumbling toward her as she slept? If they went riding together, well, I never saw him mounted much less moving. Their twin toad-brown Raleighs, dusty and webbed in the heap of our garage, seemed almost fin de siècle. Once in a while, or maybe just once, she strapped me into the vinyl seat behind her where I relaxed as she exerted, strong hips churning, before coasting into the towering tunnel of shade downhill with our arms and legs splayed spiderlike reeling pedals crushing wind crying aloud in the rude health of our decline . . .

Character

Why do some heartbreaks persist? Like an August afternoon returning home from a week's vacation in the Adirondacks when my father pulls over to the side of the road, a country dual carriageway, and parks upon the grass. Then leaves us in the car, Mother up front and the litter of us sweating in back and the nauseous wayback, as he ambles off alone along a footpath into the dappling shade of the beckoning woods. How long has he been gone? Is our engine running? When at long last he reappears, his red stainless steel canteen is full of near-freezing water from a spring. This must have been someplace from his childhood. He's not outdoorsy but there are reverberations of such manly—or boyish rather—pursuits about him. He sits at the wheel in the car and drinks his water. So pure and painfully cold—I remember to this day, so he must have allowed us a sip, though that would have been out of character. Perhaps that is why I can't forget.

Stop Sign

On the corner an autumnal Saturday after lunch an old woman is helping a young woman in sunglasses stay standing curling the woman's arm around the pole for balance as two men adjudicate one laying his hand like a blessing on her hand are they spouses has she fainted do they see in the moment where we're going

Ativan 2

Recuperating from surgery when I couldn't stand to sleep, and before the chemotherapy, when dying was impossibly likely, I had to find a way out of the house. But the catheter (my stitched-up bladder was leaking) scraped my insides like a melon baller with every wincing step toward the gleaming operating table of the Pacific at high noon. Everybody was doing whatever they could. While I yearned to cry aloud: *I am crushed beneath a storm-toppled tree. My house has fallen in upon me.* As I waited for the drug to douse my brain. Already I was tolerating; I knew I'd receive only a blossoming reprieve in which my fists uncurled. A window through which I could see myself walking.

Birthday

By the window that spies the sea, in the days before your birth, I hung the clothes you would soon wear. I knew you already. Cherished ghost of our life to come.

Wildfires

Ash drifts like pollen. A pall sieves the sun. The campfire conundrum of sage and plastic. Like the fallout from the Towers that may have sown the seeds of our tumors. There's talk of containment onscreen, maps resembling CT, PET, MRI. The waiting room's empty so the verdict is swift: "NED." No evidence of disease. The *yet* is implied, but not until some other outcome takes me hopefully while I am submerged in sleep and my daughter is old enough to write poetry for me. But for tonight we pack our bags and flee . . . In the desert morning abstractly she paints while I sketch these words for her. I drink only water. I used to sleep but now I wake at dawn. Without remorse. The bronze statue absorbs radiation. The rake is in the sand; the plunk and crinkle of phantasmal pétanque in the shade of the lemon trees while my girl sips lemonade and we debate the pros and cons of presidents and queens versus giving each other what is needed. At home the hills are rolling molten while fountains babble here. I follow my darling's darting footfalls through the flowering branches of a maze. I used to worry but now I laugh until it's gone.

The Poets' House

I keep writing about their house, I don't know why. They were old when I wasn't. This was in Providence and they were away on sabbatical in Paris. The rent was a hundred and one dollars. I had two housemates whom I hardly ever saw because both of them were in love and sleeping almost every night at their boyfriends': one who'd be diagnosed that fall with testicular, and survive, as far as I know, at least in the short term, and another who eventually dumped my housemate and she cried a lot for weeks, facedown on the poets' marriage bed. But most of that year I was alone. The walls were made of books. Burgundy velvet curtains masked the windows theatrically. Morbidly. Pull back an edge and dust would mushroom and irritate and maybe you'd glimpse an enormously overgrown elm tree, leathery green, or bare bark and edged with snow in winter. It was eerie. It's possible these old poets were clinically heliophobic. He wore a long white beard and a dirty trench coat when he went out like a cross between Gandalf and Columbo. He professed an ardor for Lovecraft. Her German accent was elegant. They collected art. My room was his study where he'd arranged on his mantle and walls framed prints of hands, like spirit photographs, some jumbled chunks of tombstones, and a painted terracotta bust of Madonna and Child beside the window as if floating luminous in the moon and streetlight watching over me suspiciously as I lay there sleepless in my sleeping bag on my futon. From the wall on the stairs the disarticulated arms of dolls reached out in hunger. Yoko Ono made and gave them a surprisingly nondescript collage. They kept Blakean printing presses in the basement beside stacks of the unsold books they'd published. Once a young poet had lived in a windowless cell in this basement, until the night terrors about being buried alive became unmanageable, and now he was living in the attic in his middle age and sometimes (though not often) I heard him stirring overhead. I have no memory of how he came and went—there must have been another door somewhere. But all of this is not what I'm thinking about which is immortality and the literary publications in that house, journals and magazines, many of which included poems by the poets from a generation or two ago. All shades of tea with age. I seldom cracked the spines. I am imagining the names listed inside. Their lives and not necessarily their words. I have my own literary publications now too, piled haphazardly on my desk and floor and shelved in almost every room and spreading, all decomposing imperceptibly yet rapidly, because where I've been living in California the danger is too much sun, and fire.

New Harmony

The town was built around two hundred years ago by Utopians—German pietists to begin with, then Scottish socialists; both movements long extinct—and in modern times it's the site of an annual convening of theatre artists, funded by an elderly local heiress of Texas oil money. Almost everybody was emoting that last night at the farewell dinner inside the renovated "old granary," the energy off-kilter like a religious revival; was something else going on? Was somebody covertly dying? Somebody always is, I suppose. Earlier in the festival an elderly actor from Chicago sat down beside me at lunch at one of those round wedding tables, misty-eyed because at his age most of his friends were gone, he explained. A young actor from Yale was getting over leukemia and at the bike rack by the rose garden he tipped me off that witches were "definitely real," he knew from experience, and they could be bad for your health. At another meal I sat beside a playwright who'd scored a commercial hit years ago, and I said something about how tough it was to survive as a writer—I was choking back tears—and he looked away muttering, "Oh, I'm sure you'll be all right . . ." Then five years later after my first batch of (mostly) disparaging reviews in New York and mere weeks after I'd been amputated from my family, a playwright said to me—we were playing cards, a whole coven of us—"Bad blood is a shame . . ." In Carol's Garden, named for the oil baroness's daughter who'd killed herself in her thirties, I sat on a wheel of local limestone beneath a net of pear tree leaves and branches, and cried for my brother twenty years after his leap. (Though he was, and is, still alive.) That year a playwright on a panel cried because no agents would represent her anymore; she'd had luck, she was tenured and endowed, even received a Guggenheim. Another playwright's Broadway debut had closed early but she waved it away over her scrambled eggs. "It's not what matters in the end." The following year my wife and I caught our breaths here on our move cross-country, parking the Penske truck on a shaded lane called Church St. Spent the night at the inn, feeling comfortably, unceremoniously middle-aged. I drank my vodka neat. Then four years pass and I'm here with a play about the ghost of a soldier. Then again recently, the summer before cancer, though I was already sick then. Drinking more. Sometime between the last and the next-to-last visit, before our daughter was conceived, I had a dream about this very house in New Harmony, where I'm writing this now. Where I hadn't stayed before having this dream. I'd been inside it once or twice. It's a house that's supposedly haunted—not necessarily benignly. And in my dream I was upstairs in the bedroom looking through the open door at a baby standing on the landing of an apparently infinitely winding set of stairs, both down and up, a child really who was raising a blind on a window and morning came streaming in before she turned to toddle toward me with her arms outstretched. Then seamlessly we were in the room together. The bright white room of life, it seemed. There was another child with us; or maybe it was the same child but older? I felt the same this morning waking up in this bright white haunted room of life: *Another child is coming.* Maybe it was the child-sized antique bed in the corner, or the child-sized antique rocking chair by the window—because how could a new child find us now? When I got in from the airport last night I found a pen on the staircase pointing at me as I climbed. I picked it up; it read: "Premier Hospice." I felt sick. But symbols are by definition changeable by reinterpretation. "The language of the soul is ambiguity," a Hollywood psychic once enlightened me, rather predictably.

Jane Owen

She was easily eighty when I met her. The white cotton dress she wore resembled a Victorian shift, as she buzzed around town in her golf cart and floppy straw hat. Her acolytes walked behind her when she walked, dressed similarly in shifts and straw hats, old but not as old as her. They'd approach you in public to press bouquets of wildflowers into your hands: "Can't keep a garden to yourself," they'd say. If they knew you wrote things with sex and violence and swear words and even slang, they might whisper through the flowers sweetly: "We will pray for you, my child." Why did I feel myself drawn toward her? Did she remind me of my mad mother? Or my mother's rich father and stepmother? Or was it a reason more sideways?—because her husband was the grandson of a senator who wrote scientifically about ghosts? Because burial mounds undulate in the verdant cemetery outside these warping windowpanes? Because not one but two Utopias failed here? Because reincarnation? And why remember her today, other than the obvious: my body has failed, or almost failed; I may be healing; I'm on a retreat here to write about grace. In any case, years ago, they sat me at her table and she gripped my hand and stared into my eyes. Probably her eyes were weak—but why *not* give an insecure young man the consideration he craves? She heard I wrote poems. She told me Yeats had not evolved: "Too bodily," she said, and that was that. We spooned our pea soup. She was whisked away. I read this afternoon—something she wrote herself—that when she came to New Harmony as a war bride she didn't expect to survive the year. She didn't write about the disease. She lived to be nearly a hundred.

Denver October

Hotels as hospitals for the (temporarily) healthy

Dancing With

The old man was menacing. After the reading. At the reception
creeping closer as he spoke. He smelled like sleep. His wife had died
two months ago of ovarian; his first wife twenty years before—ovarian
both times. Both times he'd sought solace from a Jesuit; but the old man
wasn't Catholic. He was a retired Dean of Arts. His most recent loss

had sent him pilgrimaging across Kansas and Missouri; I couldn't follow the plodding details. He followed me to dinner: "So what's *your* story?" I told him. "So what, it just went away?" He seemed to sneer. Well no, with poison and the blade. NED, I clarified. "Oh, my wives," he said, "were NED for years. I'd go on these websites, where people would say they were 'dancing with NED'—six months, ten years, 'dancing with NED'—ha ha ha!" At the end of the evening in the road as the rain fell I let him hug me, but by then I hated him.

Gethsemane

When I fear what may come I cry without sound. Mouth an O. O for olives. And the agony of the olive tree like the body gnarled and scarred but endurable, inhabited. Like insects in the wood. We scurry downhill as the sun sets with moments to spare. Reverently the tourists press against the fence that keeps the garden pristine.

Good Friday 2

Hooked on benzos, the thrice-daily benison, I am trying to remember the stations of the cross. Do I see myself, stripped and scourged, encumbered with props? I imagine Him here, at least. There are plaques in the alleys of the Old City like those in Bloomsbury and the Village memorializing even the most minor poet's briefest stay. We are dining on hummus and pita with a filmmaker upstairs in a fetid humid grotto beside the bathroom. I face the bathroom door. Our guide is describing my survival with pride; she has had cancer too. Running short on time we drive down to the Dead Sea where the sooty mud soothes and erases my scars. Then the furrowed farmlands of Armageddon; the Apocrypha will have to wait. We park and scramble up a thorny, litter-tangled hill that was the mount He sermonized from. (Disputed: there are many such hills.) I wobble queasy like a newborn foal upon the mercurial Sea of Galilee. Then skirting along the chain-link and razor-wire extremities of Lebanon, Syria, Jordan, Egypt, and Palestine—whirligigging around the axis mundi. I'm sure I'm confusing the chronology. There is no way we saw everything today. Back in Jerusalem, in the Armenian Quarter we spiral up a tower to view the sublime, leaden haze of the golden dome, while a monk plays piano below, something mournful and baroque, maybe Bach.

Wailing Wall

I don't know where we are. We are in medias res. Our benefactress lost her husband last winter to a recurrence. There are others in the car: a Jewish-atheist-feminist dramatist I've known professionally forever and a Christian filmmaker from Indiana, laboring on a screenplay about the girlhood of the Virgin Mother. Our benefactress wants us to watch a video she keeps on her phone of her husband in his final months, interviewed about how his cancer has altered his faith. Does he believe more or less? He tells a story about a morning when he was receiving his infusion and an angel was there beside him, muscular and upstanding like Saint Michael with his silver breastplate and gold lance, and how the angel spoke to him: "You must accept God's medicine." In the video as he's recounting his visitation, it's clear he believes the angel has come to assure him that he'll survive. My tongue is tied. At the Wailing Wall where I am again mistaken for a Jew, I choose not to scribble a prayer and cram it in a crevice, but to pray instead as I wrote poems as a boy in the crevice of my heart.

winter

After All We Have Been Through

Your hands warmed my naked feet in my hospital bed. Now you vent
your discontent with me. Why speak another word?

Like Abraham and Mary Todd

He's not a medical doctor, but his shingle hangs along the street where
they performed your surgery; where in a glass atrium, next to nurses
on their lunch break eating salad out of plastic clamshells, I wept when
I learned your cancer was contained. Through the winter I succored you
before we swapped roles. Now we sit cheek to cheek in a sinking couch
with arms and legs crossed in a sunset that comes boring through blinds,
listening to a stork-like old man peddle his wares. His conjugal cure.
Behind double-layered doors. "How dramatic," he remarks upon
hearing our tale: "Like Abraham and Mary Todd." How many couples
has he compared to the Great Emancipator and his grief-addled spouse?
And why? Neither of us is heroic, neither insane. I know that I am prone
to self-pity; she has her temper. Probably he says it to say something
because I can tell already we've fatigued him. His certificates are sealed
with a symbol like a cross and a trident combined. While he drones on
I'm itching to retrieve a ballpoint pen from the coffee table to transcribe
our predicament: watercolor abstractions of dancers in selected stages
of the tango; an antiquated laptop; shelves of dusty peer-reviewed
journals; a white-noise machine that's been left unplugged. This is how
we avoid asking: *Can you love me still? Can I love you still? Can you forgive
my treatment; can I forgive yours? Can we forgive our afflictions? Can rage revive
love?* We are confounded. The error is grave. In the corridor as we leave
I see what I missed on our way in: The building is old, run-down, almost
abandoned.

Suburban

Remember how we used to laugh at all the middle-aged men, husbands
and some of them still handsome, driving by in their middle-class cars
while studying you with lust? Or what we mistook for lust. We joked:

they're crashing into telephone poles, or through the living room walls of their colonial homes. We felt bad for their wives. But we took it all in our supple stride, as we strolled along hand in hand: the undeniable lure of our springtime—or yours; I don't think I thought about it much at the time. Well, I am those men now. Driving. Tender scars crawling under wraps. My stripped nerves numb. My studious pangs. Even you are beginning to disappear, you swear, my dear.

Neighbors

When we moved to Los Angeles I cold-called an agent in San Francisco who would die of breast cancer within a few years, asking for permission to write a play about her client, a shell-shocked war reporter; my wife was unemployed on account of the writers' strike, so I was about to take a teaching gig in Wisconsin alone during a perpetually blizzarding "spring term"—but I'm getting ahead of myself. That first fall I painted our screened-in porch an accidentally fecal brown and wrote out there at a scratched-up dining table (salvaged from a sidewalk in SoHo before our exodus), on a warped floor listing toward the neighbors, my plays about William James and Jesus Christ that no producer would touch with a ten-foot pole. And across the way there was another apartment with a family inside: the potbellied father in boxers and a sleeveless T, knee-high socks like Willy Loman, a browbeaten wife like Linda slumping meekly contrite while her husband berated their teenaged son who I never saw do much of anything except play shooter video games on the deep-pile shag. My writing time was consistently interrupted by the dysfunction. It was distressing, but also, if I'm honest, impressive how the boy never seemed to care—even to notice the abuse. Maybe he'd shut down? We moved. I haven't thought about them in ages. Until lately in our house where we wait and we shout and I'm wondering where they are, and if anything ever really changes.

The Dog

We had a good run. We found her fourteen years ago when she was one or three (we heard both). We knew nothing of her existence before us though she'd cock an ear apprehendingly at Spanish. We babied her because we lacked a baby then. I walked her everywhere, cut her hair; she licked herself while I wrote. Last summer I noticed her slowing down, trembling, blind and deaf or nearly. Lost. The diagnosis was lymphoma, which disturbed us. Is it the house? Why are we still living here? We opted for chemotherapy, which we could not afford really, because how could we not? She had warmed my wife's body in our bed after the mastectomies, the infusions, the radiation; she left me alone after my diagnosis, during the dismal months of my treatment, because she sensed my shame. Or she was afraid. And here we are. I drove her to the vet and read and dozed and fretted in the parked car. Then led her home: stunned and timid, like my wife after chemo, like me. Then she'd sleep all afternoon. I'd listen for her subtle breaths. She suffered a seizure one morning across the threshold of our front door. The stairs were often daunting but I pushed her, pulled her, hoping to build her up, tapping at her heels. She had her days. Nights she paced and stared through the window at the yard and the apparition of a coyote that peed upon the slates where she had peed in sunlight. Or she studied herself, the reflection she didn't recognize. Or did she? Sometimes she looked as if she were waiting to greet another dog she could see unhurriedly approaching. With the winter she declined quickly. The orbital pacing around our island. Where was she? Who were we again? Our daughter cried, anticipating the mystery. My wife and I constantly cleaning up what the dog's body no longer retained. Reminding me unfortunately of the leakage after my first surgery, my body in spasm in bed spurting through sutured holes. Still I walked her, gently pushed and pulled and lifted her in my arms. My wife fed her chicken while the technician administered the drug. I smoothed her ears. A blur leapt free of her last exhalation.

Motherless 1 & 2

Childless in my thirties in the burnt-over district in the void of winter
with my fiancée sleeping beside me in a sociopathically spartan studio
on the outskirts past the arthouse near the Kodak mansions I answered
the call from the echo of my mother, Where have you gone, Danny?
with only the bars between us; and previously in my childish twenties
in a Tidy Town in autumn warming the bench beside the graveyard until
sundown when my first love disembarked from the bus and we ascended
the back staircase past the horsey girls from Wales the boggy carpenter
from Amsterdam the coin machine cranking in the communal shower
and locked her drumskin door to devour a Neapolitan half-gallon from
the corner shop with a mangled orphan fork while I underlined *Ulysses*
in an Aran jumper and she sketched my freshly bearded face listening to
a sad song circling the drain in the pub below—that's when I noticed
through the window the toys teetering a ball a bike a doll unbelievably
in the breeze upon the landlord's moonlit roof . . .

Ativan 3

Because I am alive almost a year after treatment the doctor prescribes a
therapeutic tapering. I praise and snap the white tablet in half. The sun
is leached of light; metallic. As ever. The fountain in the courtyard runs
dry: bed of stones, no change. Paranoia refloods the brain. I am certain
they despise and defame me. If they remember me. I abhor the tenacity
of my dear demons. Is this who I am truly? I concede I am losing it yet
I demand to be heard. It doesn't matter. It's up to me to talk myself
down. Get used to this (again).

Saving Time

How is it I am here again capable of observing in passing through
windows lamps burning locks turning stoves steaming lovers kissing
each other hello as the curtains close

Sprain Road

Early evenings in winter we'd see an old woman walking relentlessly
from one end of town to the other and back again a figure of reliable
ridicule to us children how she whipped her hips elbows wrists around
bustling probably compulsively oftentimes in rain sleet snow navigating

icy sludge salt floes plowed mounds and now I know she was a survivor like me exorcising her anxiety along the red and white striating byways believing strenuous repetition might keep her future flowing cleanly believing as I do there is safety in witnessing though I do not recall her carrying a light

Movies

I haven't been here since before the cancer. In a theater, I mean. One might think it would have been an escape during treatment, but instead I couldn't face losing myself then. I wouldn't squander my time. When we were young naturally we kissed, and more. We were barely aware of the screen. We needed the cover of the story. But over the years movie theaters changed, I'm afraid, into places where I would go alone to catch my breath in the wake of conflict at home. So it is this evening with another iteration of the Great War: tracking shots prowling through gruesome trenches, the muddy suck of boots—the booming sprinkling of mortar soil like wedding rice. I cry a bit. And remember how my mother went to movies. With me. She was depressed. Somber at best, my mother hated my father. They were entrenched. In our seats before the lights dimmed she might reminisce about her mother who, during the divorce, often took my mother out of school to sit with her through a matinee, maybe two. I never knew if my mother knew what she was doing. I've never enjoyed it here really. Ever since I was a boy the lonely and deranged recognize me and comically they seek me out. Tonight in the mostly empty theater she sits with her fist in the air, clutching her twisted ticket stub. Then erupts several times about God knows what. A man stands and shouts down at her: "Would you please shut up?" She moves and sits by my side. For some reason I stay put. Will she stab me? Is she contagious? She's silent until the movie's over, then asks the pimply usher as we exit: "Have you seen this movie? No— have you actually *seen* it?"

Guilt

A born-again friend who frowned upon my profane poems and plays:
ovarian, after sixteen years of sporadic remission. Only hours after
she'd unfathomably surfaced in my mind—I was thinking about how
encouraging it was she was still alive—I learn that she has died. A tweet
in the handheld screen; my voracious feed. Then the wife of my wife's
old boyfriend, diagnosed the same year as my wife. Breast too. She lived
in Paris where her treatment was milder, my wife would often remark
with envy but also dismay. This wife would drink wine while my wife
abstained. We saw her in the summer after our cancers, her children
splashing with our daughter in the lake. She scowled, she resented
wholeheartedly. She passed away. Tomorrow's my next scan; I search
for word of a woman about my age, in treatment for almost the same
diagnosis as mine, around the same time. We kept each other company
in our reclining polyurethane seats, needles in our ports, the chemo
titrating time. Deliberating. She was the mother of three. Last I heard
hers had recurred. We emailed back and forth. She was determined,
she said, and stupefied. At some point she stopped replying and frankly
I felt relieved. And other misgivings. I discover she has been gone now
a long time. Photos of her face remain online, and photos of the sweets
she shared with family, friends, and strangers.

The Cup

I knelt knowing the napkin's caress was poetry following the golden cup
passing mouth to mouth my way and pressing my lips to the lip of the
communicable nevertheless I drank

Early Morning

I know the way. The signs are fading. The mall is liquidating. The fire station sleeps. Then turning almost somnambulistically against traffic for the shortcut, I park aboveground. Beneath laurel trees. Walk past the Afghan embassy. An old man in track pants is negotiating the stairs, the bandage on his head seeping. Security finds him charming. He sits by my side. "Up before the nurses." He winks and I reply: "We must be overeager." He's my father's age. I feel a twinge of fury that I am here too soon.

The Voices of Doctors

ring like seraphim. If minorly parental. The first replied blandly like an accountant: "Fifty-fifty," he gave me. Like Reagan or the Queen Mum, he said though he lied. Then the gruff and saturnine surgeon chewing on a nutrition bar: "We don't yet know what we may find." My wife yearned to tear his larynx out. His relief post-op; and months later with the photos, proud of his pink artistry. Then a mensch of an oncologist who was "immune to poems and plays." Pressed for stats he demurred yet always with a smile. Then the rapid-firing polymath surgeon who thought I'd been to war, who set my words to music, whose daughters I may have taught: "We can save you." "What the hell happened to you?" asked the gastroenterologist in her saucy drawl, discomfited too— "You're *my* age!" Then after the scope: "You're good to go." The nurse this morning mouths her "congratulations" in deference to the suffering surrounding us, behind sliding curtains, as she grazes my scars with gloved fingers. She hurries now because the emergency's elsewhere.

Her First Day

After her first day at the new school; after an interview on the phone concerning twenty years of writing ("I can't complain"); after learning an old friend's husband is dying with brain tumors ("Watching your feed has meant the world to us," she posts): I receive the call. "No evidence of disease." I prefer NED because remission reminds me of sin and the Inquisition. Some say "clear" like cancer's a video game or Scientology. Others say "clean" though I won't. I don't know why not. Except to say the sick aren't soiled. Not morally anyhow. I relay to my wife the news as she pushes our daughter in the swing. Our daughter is turning four next month. She swings high and leaps off and flicks me on the chin teasing—"One day you will be shorter than me!" Then lifting my shirt: "Why do you have this scar?" I stall. "This one?" Looking to her mother for rescue. The squealing swing. I pull my shirt down. "From a surgery," her mother steps in. "Doctors fixed him. Doctors went into his body and took something bad out. But he's good now. He's all good." Now my daughter has a follow-up question. "Where is your family? Not us. Your mother and father and sisters and brothers." And for the first time with her I have to justify. "I had to leave them behind." She asks, "Why? Because they were hurting you?" I am reluctant to reveal my failure twice; my weakness, at least. "Because they never learned how to love," I explain. "But please"—rushing to reassure her—"you mustn't worry, my dear. I will always be with you, I promise."

The Women

The summer after college I stayed in Vermont working for a think tank that hosted political, academic, and artistic symposia in Salzburg, Austria. Founded in the aftermath of World War II by starry-eyed Harvard students, at a certain point the organization migrated farther north. Almost everybody in the office was a woman except me, obviously. I'd sit in my cubicle all day long doing practically nothing, and if I did do anything it was to mock up the new brochure by swirling my cursor around the screen, cropping and positioning and otherwise fiddling with black-and-white photographs of intellectuals in Salzburg in the latter half of the 1940s, in a villa called the Schloss Leopoldskron where the conferences were held (the same villa that features recognizably in exteriors of the captain's home in *The Sound of Music*); and while I worked I'd listen to the women talk. About which woman was struggling. Because her husband was unemployed or depressive or cheating. About what should be "done about him." I found the gossip smothering, and tribal in a way that was probably necessary, even beneficial, but I felt defensive as a young man and sorry for the women these women were gossiping about. My supervisor was a woman who didn't take part. She seemed shy. She had two children and a husband she loved. She gave me a silver frog in a velvet pouch before I left town in August. "For your travels," she said. When I came home a year later I learned she was gone—Hodgkin's, a rare male coworker told me from behind the wheel of his car, his window rolled all the way down, looking flabbergasted in a drizzle. "Can you believe it?" He shook his head before driving away. He was a likable guy; an internet search informs me that he's gone now too.

Maybe

our bodies survive while our marriage dies

Parents Crying

Did my father cry? Impossible to imagine. Only once I saw my mother cry openly, childishly even: after my brother jumped from the window in our attic. She sobbed in my arms atop the attic stairs, instructing me: "This is a secret we must take to our graves." There were many times she'd been crying alone, hunched on the side of the marriage bed when I'd just waltz right in—just like my daughter waltzes in as I write this; and I knew like my daughter knows: my eyes are like my mother's— raw, overfull, quivering. But we don't know why, my daughter and I, do we? Are they divorcing? Does she wish she could? Is she mourning some love affair, or its lack thereof? Is she reliving some radical disfiguring (figurative or otherwise)? Does she remember her mother locking her away in a broom closet overnight for crying too long and too loudly? And how did my mother react, feeling found out like that by her son? She dried up; flustered, as I am Livid-proud. She denied by pretending, as I pretend now too. Why stain our kids with our tears? It's difficult to say anyway which inflicts the most harm, revelation or evasion. Yet in this way my mother made it clear: she did not want me crying either. The louder I cried in the crib (I suspect), the farther away she slipped. Like my wife losing her patience with me a day or two before the next chemo drip; or her inexplicable yet ineluctable anger now that treatment is over. But I digress: I never learned how to cry correctly; my tears flow copiously, occasionally, but bewilderingly because rarely do I cry about what saddens me but rather in response to countless inexhaustible obsessions concerning questions that can't be controlled or answered anyway. Recurrence. Marriage. And invariably in the dawn light I'm mortified, having forgotten the injury that inspired such lunacy. I don't feel it, you see; I simply fail to feel it. Only writing has ever helped me. As my mother seemed to imply as she handed me a pen: *You cannot cry to me so cry to them.* Yet the louder I cry, the farther away some slip. Like those who skipped town the moment they heard the word *cancer.* He'd driven through a midnight blizzard to collect me from a bus stop in Rutland; I brought a bunch of perfumed magazines to her in the hospital after her appendix burst. I married them—literally conducted the wedding! Yet who am I to judge? When a second mother to my wife lay dying of a recurrence of ovarian, I could not bring myself to say goodbye. I thought I ought to conserve my tears. We argued bitterly about that. Quiet as could be. In the night while our daughter dreamed. I hope she never wakes to hear us through the walls weeping for one of us dying, or both. Absence unending. For any reason. I pray she never has cause to read these words. Our daughter cries well though, it must be said in our defense: eye to eye, full-throated she sings; then serene . . . Unburdened. Unblamed. Maybe it's not too late to learn from her.

The Marriage Counselor

has the black crescent fingernails of the farmer the sculptor and I fear the gravedigger

The Answer

I was supposed to get married in the summer despite all the drama and I'd just had the flu, it was foggy and snowing lazily, when I was invited to a mandatory fine-dining event on the mountain in a mansion built allegedly by Al Capone, replete with escape hatches to the roof and tunnels for bootlegging. We took our seats: a promising young novelist next to his new wife, a poet; and a middle-aged writer of short stories, visiting as I was for the semester, gray-haired but simultaneously youthful like many of the childless I've known (we'd often go jogging around the same time of day, wending our solitary ways through a web of fire lanes in the forest, until one late afternoon in a sudden clearing along a ledge of mud, beside a scummy pond humming with the carcass of a stag: without a word the middle-aged writer and I passed each other and high-fived). I'd been told, before that evening, that he was a pariah on campus for seducing the young wife of a white-haired professor now many moons ago. Who knows what we discussed over dinner because nobody wanted to be there. The only thing that stuck with me was when this older writer asked the three of us: "But why would anybody *choose* to get married?" We laughed but he didn't. He wasn't genuinely asking a question. I wish I could remember what we said in response; maybe we didn't have the answer yet.

Camino Real

Because I am outraged, waylaid, I won't tell you where I am. Where the mission bell tolls and the cross condemns. Where we stole away after my first surgery in a pillar of fog and I knelt in the hotel room alone. Begging as prayer. Where we licked ice cream cones on Main St. because what else did we have to lose? Our daughter was too innocent to notice our tears (so we hoped). On the drive home I lost my breath as the road transformed into the surgeries and chemo ahead like a tunnel collapsing. It's winter now. A year and a half has passed since I was here last. On my knees again. Begging in song. No, this has been a riddle. Do you know how to find me?

Carpenteria

Three old men are sitting outside the old folks' home as the sun sets and one of them's got a theory: "Every human being is governed by fear." He goes on to list examples. I don't know if I have the courage to leave tonight, or ever. I'm reading an anthology of short stories on my laptop in my car; most of the stories are about old men dying of this cause or another. Some of the stories are funny. It's dark when the fire engine arrives, the ambulance after. Red lights flashing without sound. Parking across from me, where the old men had been sitting. I start my car when I see the EMTs unloading the gurney, taking their time . . .

In the Hotel

Ordinarily a midlife rite. Above the circus downtown. The unceasing scything of the sea. The balcony beckons, rises. I have not felt this panic since the hospital room. Or the hostel when we were young and kissed each other's feet; she was leaving in the morning and I clung to her like a steel trap. To free herself she spun the yarn of our long lives together still to come. She calls to say our daughter's worn my shirt to bed— "For the scent," she says. "She wants to know: when will you be coming home?"

Your Message

Fog the winter weather on the mountain; until out of the fog snow materializing, then evanescing into fog again: it was all so drearily mystical. And thrilling. I couldn't afford a car. I feared an SUV driven by an undergrad would come barreling around a bend in the clouds and pulverize me. So precautions were taken: hugging loose shoulders, ditch diving. This was when I began to accept the beginning of the end of youth. Events barrel past, some collide. Sickness mystifies. Sickness may clarify us yet. Every night when I made it home, unlocking the door to my borrowed fable in the woods, I rejoiced to see the blinking beacon of your message. Let me listen now.

Marriage

I fed you. You wore your helmet of ice. And mask of ice. Only a mouth opening. Mittens and slippers. Of ice. An electric blanket to maintain homeostasis. Tubes seeding your blood with the molecules that scour. Piece by piece. And I read to you, afraid of my voice, while around us the randomized populations were moaning, weeping, begging behind the curtains. I did not want to return; I had no choice. And this time you fed me.

Our Wedding

Still I feel the cream of your dress over the bone in the flesh of your hips
at the party posing in the shin-high brush with the flies scribbling around
our heads like halos disintegrating as we kissed

spring, again

Kite

Sirens for somebody. A monarch on a string. Our daughter is racing beneath its rippling tendrils. "This is the only day," she reminds us.

My Family

Sometimes I imagine you would be proud. That I have fought so hard for this life. Not that you ever cared for sound and sense. But maybe you'd respect my audacity. The fences trespassed, faces met. Secrets heard, secrets uttered. Only rarely do I wonder if, despite all evidence to the contrary, you loved me and wished mostly happiness for me and I dream of ringing you up, or better yet ringing your doorbell and surprising you with the bell-pealing laughter of the grandchild whom you can never know.

Rain

like she's never seen it. In the car we string a tune along the metronome of windshield wiping. Then score a spot near school. We wait because we're early. Looking through wet glass she asks, "Will you be dead when I'm grown up?" I remind her of Ireland. Of New England. Of everywhere we'll go. "When you die I will throw you a big party anyway," she says. I lift her as she opens her umbrella; as we approach the arroyo in the gutter: "Let me play in it," she says. *No, let me carry you across.*

Disaster 3

We were climbing out of the village through a neighborhood alpine before winding in our cautious descent into the mercantile melancholy of Yonkers—when the brakes locked, the skidding tires promising to chute us into the middle of the avenue where surely we'd be T-boned into oblivion. Mrs. Richards—malnourished, a well-manicured semi-cryptic smoker—reached out shrieking to her son who was my friend in the passenger seat. As if he could help! He was twelve and shrieking at her shrieking, seizing her seizing hand as if to say, *Me?* In the back seat I must have been frightened but I like to think I was at least a little bit amused, bracing for impact as . . . we neatly rear-ended an antiquated Mercedes-Benz. They'd been waiting at the stop sign for their chance to slip into the stream. Nobody was injured. We gathered immediately on the glassy asphalt, our fear dissipating in brief handkerchiefs of breath as we talked; the elderly couple was even laughing.

See You Next Year

I sit listening through the curtain to the chemotherapy nurses debating the meaning of the term "Irish twins," while the phlebotomist's jabbing the usual veins, then the side of my wrist, the back of my hand before she sighs, "I give up." Sopping up blood. "You won't be a hand model today. But the swelling's saline—not air—you won't *die*. Let me fetch The Vampire" . . . Who has to be of course muscular, jocular, slapping my arm—"Like your wife!" shouts The Vampire. "Doesn't your wife do this? Ha ha ha." Slap slap slap. Then: "You have a port?" I had a port. "What kind of medicine they give you?" and I have to force myself to remember: "FOLFOXIRI." She squints at me hard as if thinking maybe the treatment has worked; she doesn't say so, as she preps the other arm to plunder a virgin vein, and the initial needler endeavors to distract: "You like dogs? You have dogs? What kind? What's her name?" After the CT scan The Vampire's taping me up: "This young man is strong like a wolf!" As I gather myself to go I find the door blocked by a lamb of an old woman who's just had a scan too. She's smiling at the room full of patients in the giddiness of diagnosis, the boredom of purgation, the possibility of grace. I am inspired by the gaiety in her gaze as she says to us all, "See you next year."

Dogs Bark and I Don't Flinch

but pass by every gate. In apocalyptic Advent. A paradise is buried under mudslides yesterday; a premonition of an aftershock and mountains moving as I withdraw from the ocean in a sandstorm. The scapegoat is escaping. Inside my true form is taking shape.

That the Days

fly so swiftly is a sweetness I must try to keep even from myself

Sunset

The meaning is the scene of us clamoring to see

New Year

In the cloister of Grace Cathedral above San Francisco: a wooden chair at a wooden desk with an open book behind a leaded window. Ancient of ways. Ephemeral and more real than before.

Afterword

Maybe I'm wrong: it goes on. We inherit, we rent. Our song is made melodic with pain. Upset: cascading, respiring, ablaze. Winter's rain rinses the slight air. My daughter's hair grows while fig trees possess eternity. We illuminate each other: The hummingbird eats the spider. Coyotes digest the genius of crows. Animals are animals. And so on. "And the spaceship swallows the whale?" She thinks this is the end. Yes, I surprise her, as we fly away to another planet.

ACKNOWLEDGMENTS

14: "Dedication"

32 Poems: "The Poets' House"

Ambit: "Her First Day," "The Voices of Doctors"

America: "Marriage"

Bad Lilies: "The Answer," "B—"

Bennington Review: "Motherless 1 & 2," "Prometheus"

Birmingham Poetry Review: "Disaster," "Flying on Easter," "Genetics," "Good Will," "Lazarus in Remission," "Napping after Cancer," "Passports," "Sunday," "They Look at You," "A Vision"

Blackbird: "Anger," "Disaster 2," "A Nurse's Tattoo," "On Symbols"

Briar Cliff Review: "Bikes"

Cincinnati Review miCRo: "Good Friday 2"

Cortland Review: "Carnivorous"

Cyphers: "The Parting Glass"

Exacting Clam: "Afterword," "Ativan," "Ativan 2," "Ativan 3," "New Hampshire," "Past," "Sprain Road," "Use"

Fenland Poetry Journal: "Movies," "See You Next Year"

The Fiddlehead: "Birthday," "Fish Market," "Forever For Sale," "Our Wedding," "Shared Wall," "South," "Stop Sign," "Whether"

Greensboro Review: "Guilt"

Hopkins Review: "Alma Mater," "Carpenteria," "Dancing With," "Evening Echo," "Funny," "Good Friday," "Jane Owen," "Labor Day," "Unpublished," "The Women"

Laurel Review: "Like Abraham and Mary Todd"

Magma: "Headshots"

The Moth: "Now," "The Nurse"

New England Review: "After Borges"

North American Review: "Gethsemane," "New Harmony," "New Journal," "New Year," "On Time," "Pride," "Reminder," "Saving Time," "Sunset," "That the Days"

Northwest Review: "New Hampshire 3," "Worry"

Plume: "Early Morning," "Fragment," "Kite," "Neighbors," "Parents Crying," "Therapists"

Poetry Birmingham Literary Journal: "The Dog"

Poetry London: "Rain," "Wildfires"

Poetry Salzburg Review: "Aliens," "Our Mother's Health"

Raceme: "Disaster 3," "Forgiveness," "In Time for the Lesson"

Southern Review: "Perseverance"

Southword: "French Press"

A Story That Happens: "Character"

Sugar House Review: "After the Scan," "Fire Escape," "New Hampshire 2," "Secondhand"

Under the Radar: "I.M. M.P.," "The Toothbrush," "Why Write"

Wild Court: "The Chair," "Life Will Be Harder," "The Prize," "Save Oneself"

Witness: "The Crab"

I wish to thank the New Harmony Project, and artistic directors Mead Hunter, Lori Wolter Hudson, and David Hudson, for providing me with a writing residency in New Harmony, Indiana. My thanks also to Cindy Bayer and the Writers' Gathering for bringing me to Israel. And lastly my gratitude to Acre Books and the insight and support of editors Lisa Ampleman and Nicola Mason.